Series Quatre

The little book

I0396857

Environmental

Analysis

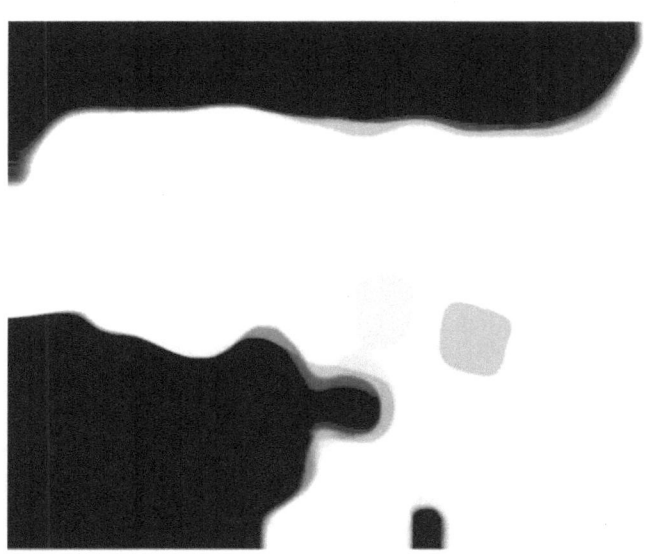

Lawrence Michael

an presentation 2016 revised edn.

ISBN 10: 1514392240 ISBN 13: 978-1514392249
cover jacket –inside cover & other illustrations by the author

Typeset in Cambria

To you. Seriously!

Contents

Preface 7

Using this book 13

Chapter one *What is Environmental Analysis?* 16

Chapter two *EA or Environmental Analysis* 30

Chapter three *Starting with EA* 34

Chapter four *Proxemics* 46

Chapter five *Change* 53

Chapter six *Terrorism: Should One Worry?* 66

Chapter seven *Dealing with Changes of All Kinds* 79

Chapter eight *The Clash of Claims & Opinions* 84

Chapter nine *Welfare States* 90

Chapter ten *Deriving Our Action Plans* 96

Selected References 109

The heart of your business lies in minding

it well.

They do not seem so very simple when you begin looking at it seriously. From a viewpoint of strategic success of your business, it makes sense to take a snapshot view of the various factors that affect your life & living. Crucial, since business is merely one important dimension of it. So I do hope that we remain clear about that and understand that much of the complexities come from human creations, of which both trade & commerce are as much of human creations as your comprehension of life & living too is. Before one ventures further, let us first understand what the term strategic success in business means. Perhaps you would find that it is not very different in life & living either! The two terms define our commonsensical outlooks:

1. Tactical: Tactical is the word used to describe short term objectives or goals in any endeavour. It usually means that you would probably be planning for your marriage when you are eighteen or twenty. Marriage is a serious issue and needs a lot of planning if you are serious about it, with the first usually being your job. Well, some may say that it should probably be started by the time you reach puberty, and take the fun out of your teen years.

2. **Strategic**: Strategic is the word we use to describe long term objectives or goals in any endeavour. That means that you probably need not take the fun out of your teens but definitely need to plan a little ahead about your life after marriage, if not only just before it. That would mean planning to make the marriage a success (both before and after having your children) and also planning for your children too, if the meaning of marriage for you & your partner also includes children.

Next we need to use the two terms in manners that allow our thinking to be for a clear plan. Now we do plan for most things in life. Planning could easily be termed as being *tactical* or *strategic* depending upon how far into the future are we really planning for. The reason why the two terms are often used in many situations, including that of business ventures help in our better usage of the two ordinary concepts. Well, the moment one hears of planning, one probably also has heard about the basics of business & organization that the acronym PODSCORB stands for. It becomes clearer in both the logic of certain basics as well as the value-structures that it embodies. PODSCORB is something that Luther Gullick invented and it has been immensely popular ever since. It is a concept and a tool.

EA uses PODSCORB as a tool – in fact a very critical tool in analysis of groups, states & societies, amongst a great variety of resources. The reason why PODSCORB is so interesting and invigorating a tool of analysis is simply because nearly every school going children has read about it, before they entered college or universities.

The interesting part is – that includes policy-makers and other responsible people that one often read about in newspapers, etc. – are included in those batches of school-going children. They can't deny it, or defend their decisions to stand in for public offices if they haven't heard of some basics in organization.

So one supposes that we shan't be expecting shoddy public places including roads, and their environments, including law & order at all. Know of a place that is nothing but *merely just that shoddiness?*

So even if we, as young adults, are stepping onto a place – we have every right to assume that it already has been PODSCORB-treated by the preceding generations. Our task is then as simple as improving and bettering that what we have inherited. Is it not? Brilliant if we extend the same natural expectation to every sphere of public life – including business ethics.

One supposes that one need not really break one's head over how organized individuals are in their private lives – apart from the fact that it is no one else's business to begin with, as long as they do not begin spilling their private lives onto the streets and adversely affect the quality of public life that we all have an equal right to – as a *common good*. There! Having PODSCORB as your easy-tool-of-analysis is what empowers the layperson – to make your own judicious judgments about people and places that may interest your investment instincts. We just have begun on EA.

Lawrence Michael

This book is your DIY guide to life, living and of course business investments. Designed as a simple guide for investors, small businesses and the ordinary lay person, this book offers you simple tools for insightful views to help you analyze your own environments as well as those of others.

The first chapter takes you through to the next. Using the familiar POSDCORB of Luther Gullick to build up, the other chapters introduce you to the simple processes involved in making judicious decisions. A near fool-proof methodology, EA helps you organize your own personal life better. Most chapters are littered with wisdom-pearls that are pragmatic, and help you move towards intelligent decision-making. The to-do list at the end of most chapters helps you get a practical grasp of the idea discussed in the preceding chapter.

It is also a handy-guide to serious policy-makers that would like to cut through the paper-works over development project reports and get to the truth as easily and simply as it is lived, outside the paper-world and obvious smoke & mirror exercises that governance mean for many states and regions of the world. Thus helping seek accountability while making themselves accountable.

Added as a priceless extra, the chapter on *Dealing with Change of All Kinds* helps the average reader and ordinary communities, groups and societies secure themselves better – should governmental apathy mark their states and/or regions. The book is designed to make for easy comprehension and has tried to cut through most of the esoteric jargons employed. Given that environments matter, the book has dealt with the difficult topic of crime & terrorism, as it also introduces the reader to the basics within discussions and debates that otherwise seem far too *specialized* and thus esoteric.

Go through each chapter first and then take upon the to-do list at its end. Once you are sure that you have understood both the theoretical as well as the practical dimensions of the topic, move on to the next chapter. It is advisable if you do so only when you feel comfortable with the level covered. The last chapter concludes by introducing you to the basics of research methodology as well as data – so that you comprehend better their functions and are not overwhelmed when presented with a complex set. Additionally, having already covered some practical aspects of those by now, you can finish the book with more or less a basic expertise in the matters of analysis and pragmatism. From a layperson to a basic expertise – this is what this book helps you achieve in the everyday common language as well as sensibilities. Happy reading!

Reading is a beautiful habit. It
never is a burden to read one
book once or twice for a once
better comprehension than
having read many books minus
one.

Reading as an art.

Chapter One

What is Environmental Analysis?

What is an Environment?

The word environment immediately, and commonly, conjures up visions of something to do with the ecology; or the physical natural environment. But environment is social and political as well. Environment is cultural as well in certain milieu. Environment is also business and economic.

So we do use the term environment with reference to many situations and contexts. They can and do refer to various milieus within a particular geographical location, including the *meaning* of ecology. They can and do refer to the various milieus, in various *and* different geographical locations. With EA or Environmental Analysis, we take into account the various environments that we so often do speak about, apart from the ecology or the natural physical environment.

The basic kinds

Simply put, we do come across two broad kinds of environments that we refer to:

First is the commonly understood meaning of environment as the physical & natural environment around us. This refers to our climate, water, trees, plants & air. It also refers to the outer-space and includes that as part of its concerns when we do speak of environment as ecology.

Second, we refer to *human* social-cognitive environments when we speak of the various environments at hand. We refer to human environments when we speak of cultural or social or political or economic or even business environments. This remains distinct from the natural physical-natural environment that we call ecology, or refer to the planet earth for its formative set of conditions that are necessary for our natural existences.

What are we referring to?

When we refer to the term Environmental Analysis or EA, we are referring to both the set of environments and to their interplays. In other words, we are looking at the various environments that the Human world throws up, and their impacts upon the natural environment as well the human socio-cognitive worlds – when planning for business. As well as for life!

EA or Environmental Analysis helps you with simple tools and markers that can help you comprehend and easily analyze any given human environment. Now we know that human environment, like the natural-physical environment, is a very diverse one. Both business & politics (or even your ordinary life or *la vie quotidienne*) is greatly affected by the diversities in the human social-cognitive worlds. These diversities mark the various Human Environments, amidst all its richness and diversities and form crucial areas where an identification of what would suit us strategically is all the more important and crucial.

> Always appreciate differences and
> diversity that are presented as
> cultural and/or religious.
> Appreciation does not mean an
> acceptance though it may help you
> in being accepted.
> Crime is never a diversity and
> always a burden.
>
> *Appreciating diversities*

It thus involves a rich source of data that we do need to use specialized tools to simplify and render tangible. In a globalized world, the importance of having a sound and correct understanding of the various human environments remain imperative. In fact, the importance of an effective EA or Environmental Analysis, can never be emphasized more than in today's worlds, and realities of diversities that come from globalization as a process. Including immigration.

Appreciating Diversities

Is it not quite a *potpourri* of diversities already in your local town or city – even if you are a community of people of the same race, belief & social background? It already is a *potpourri* of environments if you simply take into account that what you would call the cultural environment of your town or city. You would be referring to the political environment as well as the economic environment.

You would even be referring to the law & order situation of your town or city: *as an environment* by itself. Many do or we do count it as crucial in affecting/determining the other environments – cultural, economic, social, educational, etc. So right here, in this imaginary situation, we find diversities as well as the recognition that data is not simply about the demography of your town or city. It is also about the quality of it that is immediately affected by, say, the law & order situation, or environment of your town and/or city.

Does it not matter about what kind of civic amenities you have in your town or city, apart from the law & order situation/environment, before you or a visitor to your town would classify it? Including the quality of the water in the river that flows by, and the quality of the air that you breathe?

a. How does one differ?

1. Differing is easy when you know what you are differing from. This remains a crucial area for me. Very often we may tend to differ just because it seems clever to do so. Or sometimes just because it is possible to do so.

2. Those urges of *wanting* to be clever without being intelligent remain a strict No-NO for me. Differing is again not easy in the real sense because you are pitting your mind against those already there. They have not been there without a reason. It helps to know – then – why you are there in the first place.

3. Answering this one **First Step** helps in saving everyone a lot of money, and time.

4. Environmental Analysis takes into account Human Behaviour that is seen at convergence/divergence with Human Behaviour flowing out from the First Principles as briefly explained here: conditions of negative peace & positive freedom as the basic minimum standard bearers of conditions in any society and/or state.

5. It studies states and societies at the basic physical markers of organized/planned living that their public living spaces demonstrate and acknowledge. The mind-

scape or psycho-cultural roots for conflict & violence form the other crucial markers that are immediately visible in the public life. The notion of societal conflict (both direct and indirect violences) and their occurrences as well their resolutions are important markers for the health of any society and include issues of transparency, governance & honesty indicators.

b. Differing-in-care

Differing in topics such as multi-culturalism & migration can be very sensitive as well as tricky topics. They are fraught with some conceptual mind fields. It makes it more difficult when you are faced with policy-makers who may be new on their jobs or a rank outsider to the subject. Or the issue areas you are talking about involve changes at a strategic level.

Factors:
1. Structural Factors
2. Psycho-cultural factors
3. Deep-Cultural Imperatives
4. Mediation between Structure & Deep Culture matrices.
5. Genesis of Psycho-cultural Factors.
6. Discursive Analysis & Media

SAINTS LOUIS, GEORGE AND   LES SAINTS LOUIS, GEORGES ET
MARGARET   MARGUERITE
(*Doge's Palace, Venice*)   (*Palais ducal, Venise*)
DIE HEILIGEN LOUIS, GEORG UND MARGARETE
(*Venedig, Dogenpalast*)
D. Anderson, Photo.

52

SAINTS ANDREW AND JEROME   LES SAINTS ANDRÉ ET JÉROME
(Doge's Palace, Venice)   (Palais ducal, Venise)
DIE HEILIGEN ANDREAS UND HIERONYMUS
(Venedig, Dogenpalast)
D. Anderson, Photo.

b

One is Careful in EA when one sets out with the basics of carrying out any analysis. One can never emphasize the importance of taking extreme care when determining what forms data, including their generation. In other words qualitative & quantitative methodologies both remain crucial to data determination, collection as well as analysis. Where EA goes one step further is by beginning from the basic foundational positions of the limitations inherent in the various *episteme* that are available or contend in the world and accepts and tries keeping itself updated above the various ontological positions and assumptions and their respective validations. Comparative study is made with previous data and divergences explained for. Comparative study of various Cultural & Cross-Cultural Groups; Comparative Psychological Studies of Value-systems and Goal Orientations; Comparative Psycho-Cultural Study of various risk groups across the globe.

a. Each study also studies their environments and their respective positioning/placements vis-à-vis others within their given similar/familiar environment. Analysis is done over what explains and mediates the relative success or failures of those studied.

b. A comparative analysis with their environments is juxtaposed with comparative studies of other environments across the globe.

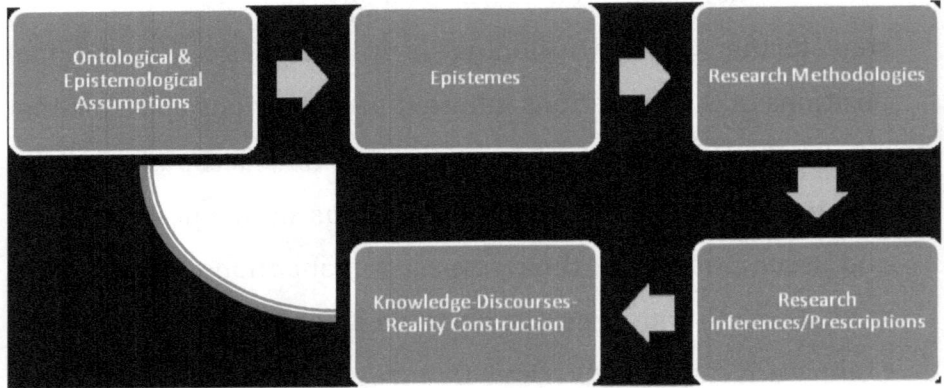

a. *The Basic Process in Reality Construction and what informs (affects) which*

b. Basic Flow of Knowledge Systems or Epistemes

How EA differs:

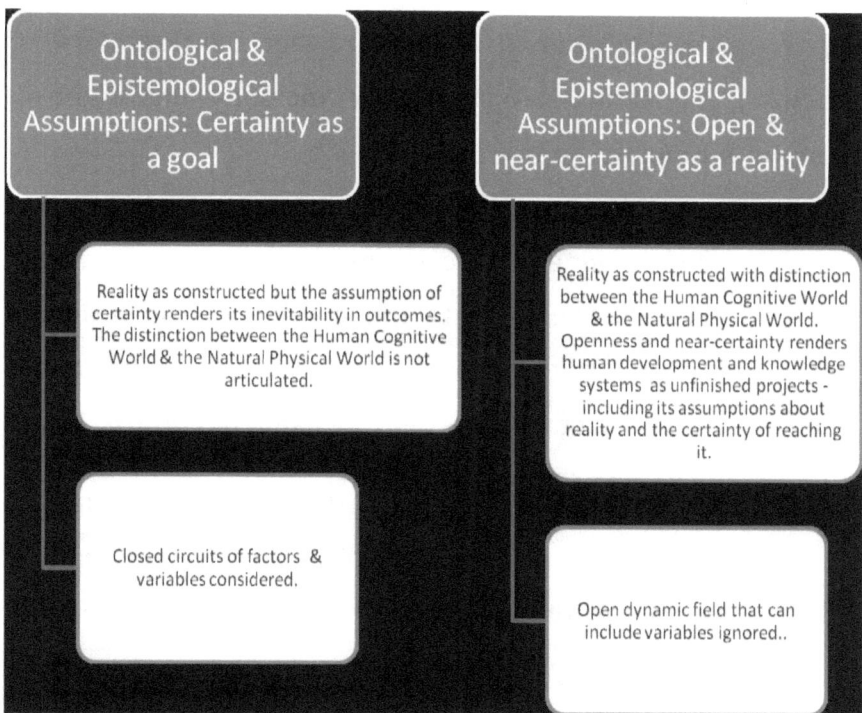

b. Basic Differences between ordinary Epistemes & Environmental Analysis.

c. Establishing the First Principles

Life, Living, Value-Systems, Individual Freedom, Human Rights (First Principles & Human Rights are not contradictory or conflictual), Right-to-Life-With-Dignity includes the Right-to-Livelihood & Equality-before-Law.

    a. Town-Planning: We take care of our physical environment and civic amenities are primary amongst those. This extends to the rural areas as well and strongly marks societies and cultures as repositories of their societal values/features and/or culture.

    b. Civic Rights: Civil Rights and the issue of Freedom are crucial markers since our physical space is marked and meant for our cognitive-emotive existences and are marked by civil rights.

    c. Conflict Resolution: Levels of conflicts in any given society and the most preferred modes of conflict resolution are important markers for the political & cultural health of any society.

How is Change viewed in the EA?

The first difference in other studies that deal with the subject of change (Future Shock by Alvin Toffler remains a popular best-seller of its times) and that of EA is that in EA it is considered important to comprehend what are the factors that cause change, than merely studying the impact of change on human life and value-systems.

Given our earlier recognition of the constructed nature of human reality (and the useful distinction that the English philosopher Roy Bhaskar helped elucidate between the natural, physical world and the human social-cognitive world), we realize that we are the agents of change in our lives. This recognition helps us find a greater sense of control in our lives and it is not an erroneous assumption either. Or even merely a figment of one's imagination that gets blown in thin air the moment one puts it to scrutiny. This recognition helps us deal with the factors of change better – knowing that each factor is a human creation in the human world (one is leaving out natural events out from our analytic scope for now – since they are natural forces or factors of change – like an earthquake, for example and our better organization helps us have that already factored in when we do build our houses or towns and cities). Isn't it? What we are doing with EA as a tool is comprehend our human worlds better. Thus be in a better control of our own destinies, as such.

Each study is compared against the *First Principles* already established as the ideal conditions that remains constant. What causes the divergences? For example, what would be change seen here? Change in the social, political, economic & cultural factors/characteristics of any given society/community, and/or state is seen very simply against a few basic set of questions. Did you know that these basic set of questions are also known as the Journalist's standard guide in asking questions? Great, is it not? That it always has been so well known and is so simple actually!

Here they are:
What? Where? When? How? Who? Whom? Why?

Now when you do investigate CHANGE in any state or society, it is very easy to also see it in the light of some basic periods.

1.   **Day-before-Yesterday:**

What was there? Where was it? When was it? How was it? Who did it? Why was it done? To whom was it done?

2.   **Yesterday:**

What was there? Where was it? When was it? How was it? Who did it? Why was it done? To whom was it done?

3.   **Today:**

What is there? Where is it? When did it appear? How is it? Who has done it? Why has it done? To whom is it been done to?

Knowing them should be able to tell you what may be possible *Tomorrow* and the *Day-after Tomorrow*. Yes? Yes! Of course! Remember that we aren't studying the impacts of change but change itself in our lives. Moreover, to help us actually *change* our lives for the better.

Things to do:
1. Make a list of the various different ethnicities that make up your village, town and/or city.
2. Make a list of the different kinds of religious faiths that are practiced in your village, town and/or city.
3. Make a list of the different kinds of vegetation found in your area.
4. Make a list of the different kinds of animals (both wild and tame) found in your area.
5. Make a list of the different kinds of feathered friends (birds) in your area.
6. Now make a list of the number of hospitals for humans and non-humans in your area.
7. How would you rate compassion towards non-human life forms in your area:
   a. Excellent   b. Very good
   c. Good.   d. Average   e. Poor   f.   Very poor.

Chapter Two

EA or Environmental Analysis

> Listen carefully to what is said around you. Even at social gatherings. Listening is an invaluable art that always helps. Give others the attention that you would have sought. If not, give them the attention they seek.

Listening is important

Environmental Analysis or EA is a simple tool that we use to improve both our lives and businesses. It does so by *simply* recognizing that business and life are both very responsible ventures. They both need careful planning & responsible living.

Environmental Analysis or EA merely helps you find this confluence easily. You would be using simple everyday examples and models in your life to help you find better planning and strategic security for both your business, and your life. They are not very different and with EA you will also be perhaps encouraging your friends and neighbours to try the EA approach. Just like you spell it and pronounce it – it means an analysis of the environment.

1. Environmental Analysis helps you get a comprehensive picture of any business/investment destination as well as evaluate your own domestic environment in a better comparative manner. It is a easy Do-It-Yourself business tool.

(It is a secure tool for small enterprises as well as to the large corporations & global conglomerates. It is easy to see why it works so effectively and so well for such a wide range of industries as well as helping you achieve a better life and *quality of living!*)

2. Get an easy but effective structural to psycho-cultural (and the deep culture) analytics of any destination. The insights offered are invaluable for the strategic interest of any business/

investment. This is because it also explores the possibilities of developmental work and *environment up–gradation* of any place that strategic business investment destinations mean in effect. This helps you plan your project with a better strategic success and societal/community development plans.

But what is it?

Starting Now

Let us start with a first step. Know of the POSDCORB logic invented by Luther Gullick? Many school-going children or even early college-going young people may have read about the acronym. Common to the subject of *Public Administration*, it involves the basics of any organizational functioning. It, of course, also contains a certain logic or *rationale.*

A *rationale* that accrues from certain solid foundational values that imagine how any organization is meant to be organized. When we think of organization, we also are thinking of maximizing of returns with a minimal of inputs.

Or what we call investments with a high returns. Simply because when we do get organized, we get organized to get something done. Usually for a long term or what we term as strategic goals; and sometimes also for the short-term or what we call the tactical goals.

STEP ONE: Take your camera and go out. Record the life on the roads and the streets. Now any state and society too is an organization. What do the streets, people and their basic interactions and values tell you about that place? When simply compared with the school-goer's knowledge of Gullick's POSDCORB logic? There you go!

> One of the keys to success is being well-prepared for any situation. Being well-prepared comes from having anticipated before. Be it your data, information and/or situations.
>
> *A key*

Chapter Three

Starting with EA

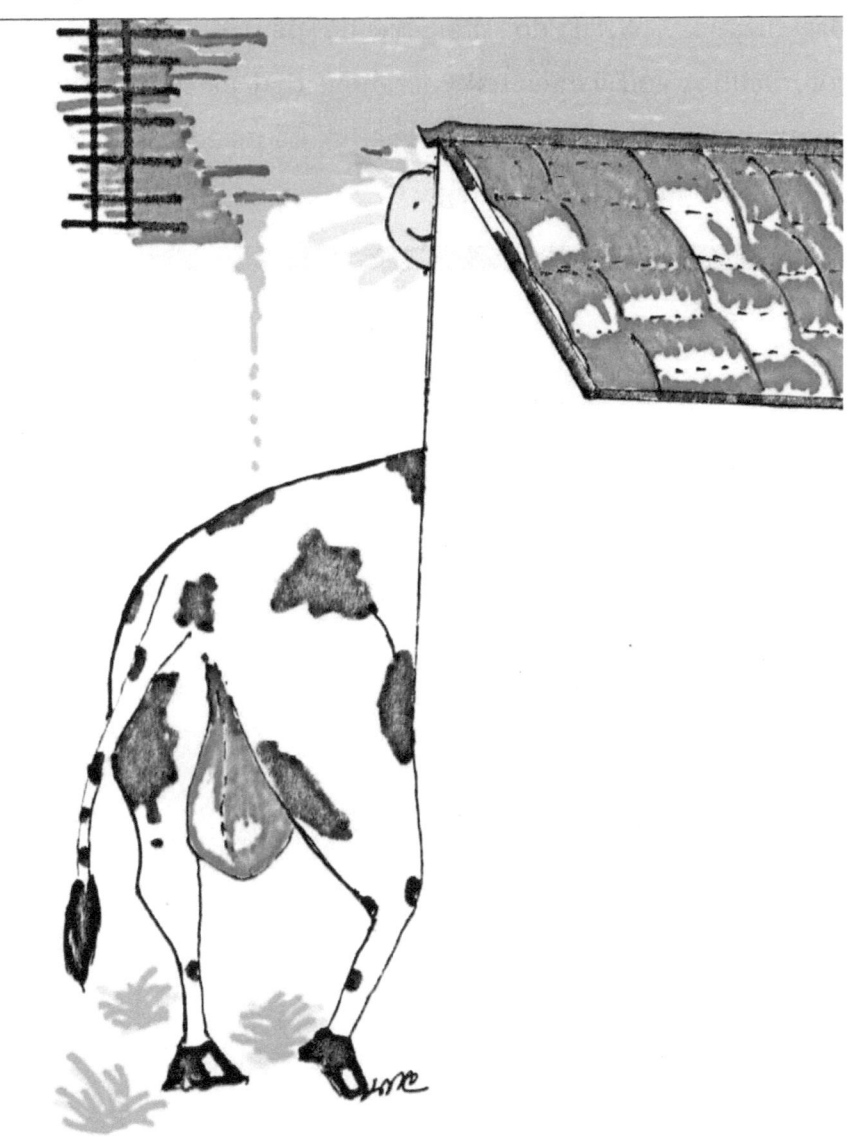

Re-discovering Public Administration

We know that POSDCORB is an acronym. An acronym is the shortening of a long name or concept using its key alphabets to make a word that we easily use to remember it. It actually is an abbreviation.

P O S D C O R B

P = Planning: The first step of thinking about any enterprise: what is it? How should it be? How do we go about effecting it?

O = Organizing: The second step in thinking about any enterprise: Have we got the necessary resources & conditions for it?

S = Staffing: The third step in thinking about any organization: Have we got the necessary skills & dedicated people to handle all the responsibilities that accrue in the wide-ranging tasks required?

(Have we successfully secured all the positions with the correct personnel? I obviously would not ordinarily hire a chef who specializes in making food to look after finances.)

D = Delegating: The fourth step in thinking about any enterprise: it involves the streamlining of responsibilities and creating the workflow chart based upon staffing needs and specializations/skills of the personnel.

CO = Co-ordinating: The fifth step in thinking about any enterprise: How do we get all the varied tasks delegated to function towards achieving the stated objective of the enterprise?

R = Reporting: The sixth step in thinking about any enterprise: How do we keep a tab upon all the personnel and tasks and get our timely updates & reports upon their status?

B = Budgeting: The seventh step in thinking about any enterprise: How do we allocate the resources towards the various tasks involved that finally end up as the end-objective? This necessarily includes salaries and payments made towards outsourcing as well as in-house tasks.

Now let us look at the POSDCORB acronym with a little more detail. After we look at it, we shall briefly touch upon *proxemics* in the next chapter to see how it impacts our parameters of analysis that we shall be taking on as the first simple DIY analytics of the EA. We necessarily shall take another look at *proxemics*. Meanwhile, we shall look at POSDCORB a little more.

Always ask yourself the reason for doing something. When something seems more a habitual activity, avoid entering into it. This includes making decisions to please someone else – unless it involves your winning the Nobel Prize or some other honour/riches.

Always enquire

POSDCORB detailed

1. Planning entails the basic necessary planning that you go into before undertaking any project. Planning is intrinsic to any of our endeavour and is involved even when we go out for plain shopping. It involves a prior estimation of what is needed for any given project or task, and thinking of all the necessities. For example, even when we cook a dish, we plan for it and get all the required ingredients and conditions in place before cooking it. So even if it is a salad that we plan to make, we would need all the ingredients as well as the chopping board, and the necessary sets of cutting utensils or knives before we launch ourselves for it. Many things seem common-sensical because we have planned for it. Planning thus needs some prior knowledge or we would be left with all the ingredients for a salad without a knife or sets of knives, and maybe even the chopping board!

2. Organizing entails getting all the ingredients together at the place of execution. So for making a salad, we would need the ingredients and the chopping board with the knife, or a set of knives before starting making our salad. Is it not? What organizational structure you would select for yourself is largely dictated by 1. Your objective or reasons for an organization. 2. Your strategic planning. This in turn depends upon how well informed you are about the various environments that you will deal with.

3. Staffing is a critical part of any enterprise. This is simply because we cannot do everything ourselves. Any organization typically needs a minimum of personnel to carry out its various tasks. Even if we outsource most of our tasks, we still would need a minimal number of personnel to man the office and regulate and organize the outsourcing, including the vital decisions of what needs to be outsourced and where. Staffing remains critical even if outsourcing solves most of our problems and helps us maximize our cumulative outputs.

Staffing is critical

4. Delegation occurs after staffing and which occurs after organization and which occurs after planning. After any organization has its set of personnel – they will include a hierarchy in terms of position and responsibilities. These in turn necessitate the need for delegating the tasks. Delegation simply means dividing the tasks at hand amongst the various personnel – in whose share a particular task and its responsibility falls and has to be met. That becomes his/her job at hand and we pay him/her his remuneration/salary based upon the degree of responsibility any individual bags in the delegation process.

5. Co-Ordination is the task of synchronizing the various tasks and delegated responsibilities amongst the various personnel to achieve the stated given objective at any time. If making a salad is the task at hand, various personnel responsible for the procurement of the ingredients, as well as the chopping board and knives will need to be co-ordinated to get them on time and at one place.

6. Reporting is an intrinsic part of any organization and refers to the status-update about each and every tier and/or level and their performances so that the organization is able to know how far and in what manners (crucial) it has moved towards achieving its any given objective.

7. Budgeting is intrinsic, even if mentioned last. Each and every task or procurement costs money and resources, including the personnel employed. Even when we are outsourcing a task or job, it costs money and/or resources. The allocation of specific resources/money to the various departments/segments for carrying out their tasks is what we call budgeting and usually includes the costs of employment in it.

> Never offer to do something in haste. It saves you from the trouble of a shameful withdrawal later.

Haste is waste

Using this POSDCORB logic

Having understood the POSDCORB acronym, its logic becomes easy and obvious. It is to increase efficiency in any given enterprise as well as task where the output is sought to be maximized when compared to the input. The rationale is to eradicate wastage and obviously inefficiency and thus crime as well.

Getting On with practical EA

Now let us take our Environmental Analysis task at hand. You will see how an easy DIY range it covers. To begin with:

a. You would be looking for and identifying places that serve as public spaces. Public spaces are long term affairs and include the roads, streets and the sidewalks, including the drainage systems and other basic public utility services like supply of potable water, electricity, telecommunications and law & order environment of any town or city or a place.

b. You would be comparing their status and performances through the POSDCORB logic that tells you of their planning and execution and if the current load is well within the planned limits.

c. You will examine their reception by the people for whom it has been planned. Abuse and destruction of any public utility service indicates the anti-state/criminal elements in any location and immediately tells you of the crucial law & order environment of any state. Law & order are not about just violent crimes. They also are about a civic sense that is at once visible in any village, town or city. It is crucial because no state can expect to perform without its populace accepting it and whose degree is immediately visible in the public utilities as well as the public services available there.

d. You will then simply compare the life of the affluent, the middle-class and the poorer sections of the populace to check their receptions of the state, as well as their receptions by the said state in question. Any state with a pre-dominant poor reception either way means a poor legitimacy. Critical for the success of your living as well as your business environment.

e. Finally, of the first stage, you'll examine if available (you need not go looking for it) those elements that go out to make the state more legitimate or more illegitimate, as the case may be. Between the two, you'll immediately discover if that place is suitable for your stay should you plan an extended one! Or not. Any place that does not attract you to extend your stay for the positive reasons is a straight negative.

Things to do:

State – Citizens – State Employees

1. What are the factors that lend to a state's particular performance(s) at the level of public utilities?
2. What are the reasons behind the particular receptions of a state by its populace, and their (populace) receptions by the state (state-employees themselves are citizens of the state)?
3. What are the reasons for any variations, if any, for receptions at the two directions across the three levels of any place's populace?
4. How much is the state's behaviour gendered/sexist – at its all public levels of interactions and functioning?

•*A* starter's EA Key

Any investment is your plant. Watch your sapling grow into a huge tree. It is a rich experience to be eco-affirmative just as you are life & profit affirmative. Know that EA Values keep your business and life on the upswing, even when business seems in a down turn. That is because EA upholds values & common sense together; making the task of describing *what is commonsensical?* much more fun and life-positive!

Chapter Four

Proxemics

> Never mix business with pleasure,
> no matter how attractive they
> both may seem together.

The basics

Human behaviour has long occupied human concern. It also is intrinsic to management and business in case you thought only psychologists and social scientists thought about it! The book *Social Encounters: Readings in Social Interaction*, edited by Michael Argyle forms a rich collection of essays. It, however, remarkably begins with a 1968 article by Irven DeVere headed *Primate Behaviour.* The introduction states that this is a companion volume to the earlier book *Social Interaction* by Michael Argyle.

Within the rather placid start – the development of the topic remains one of the more engaging aspects within human behaviour – where we engage ourselves with *proxemics* – whose definition the second article provides by Edward T. Hall who innovated the term. *Proxemics* is defined as "the study of how man unconsciously structures microspace – the distance between men in the conduct of daily transactions, the organization of space is his houses and buildings, and ultimately the layout of his towns."

Proxemics thus naturally holds our attention as a tool that can help us organize human settlements better to reduce conflicts, and help design create the human *Utopia.* It also then helps us identify pathologies or groups exhibiting those – and thus identify the macro-conditions (as original outcomes & later environments?) or particular *anti-cultures.*

We find that a negligence in those aspects when designing our villages, towns and cities exhibit a far more serious lacunae than a mere absence of the POSDCORB logic, because it also entails a confession of a cavalier attitude and a non-reception of both positions of authority as well as the people – for whom we ostensibly design public places as well as villages, townships and cities. The absence of the POSDCORB logic would present a criminal organization at place, or a plain incompetent one.

We can thus find *proxemics* help us identify and even classify groups and individuals more prone to pathological behavioural dysfunctions, as well as violence. This emergence of *proxemics* as a tool for criminology makes it an attractive tool for studying terrorism as well – given the functional attributes of the two as cognate concepts.

Finding where it is

We find that we actually function around two sets of assumptions. One is the derivation of *proxemics* as a set of values that we configure around human behaviour that we seek to derive from the environment-nature-adaptation concepts that Darwinism would push forth. We find a start in that in *Primate Behaviour.* The second set seems to veer around our assumptions about human behaviour and their developments into the various cognitive universes that we also tend to refer to as *cultures.*

This is seen in the study of varying *proxemics* that the second chapter of the book *Social Encounters* edited by Michael Argyle posits – where we find an introduction to the term *proxemics*. It remains interesting in studying the emergence of the various *proxemics* that we find ourselves with – where we do examine their climactic conditions to derive their reasons and conditions for organizing their space as they have done – if at all.

Often haphazard and arbitrary structures can be thrown up as examples of *proxemics* and which aren't those but merely reflect more an absence of thought than any planned settlement of humans. However it remains obvious by now that technological advancements have played an important role in how we undertake the planning and organization of our living spaces, including their execution. This affects the *proxemics* of any group but does not replace ignorance, wilful neglect and/or criminal disregard that often may seem to afflict some human settlements more than others.

The newer challenges

Both the approaches – the one that focuses upon *primate behaviour* to comprehend human organization of their spaces, and the cultural outgrowths that we refer to as the various cognitive universes/cultural cosmologies however, figure in as approaches. This then bring us to a complex maze of considerations in looking at human behaviour – where the term

American would definitely set it apart from the term *Arab* – given the rather recent emergence of the *American* from Europe. The consideration of an *American proxemics* then reduces the time-span we consider for involuting environment-nature-adaptation matrix in determining the *proxemics* of any group.

It also sets us the task of analyzing if the various cosmologies have emerged from the various *proxemics* given that space and its organization do have a critical impact upon human thought, as well as evolution as *beings.* Juxtaposed with their environments (particular groups may display differing organizational patterns as well as adaptations. Eg. Not everyone in the cold climes have taken to *Igloos*), we often include their access to technology to ascertain their adaptation methods as well as the ranges of it.[1]

One the other hand we find Johan Galtung put forth a very interesting proposition that he calls the *deep culture* or the *cosmology. Deep Culture* is defined as "the 'collective subconscious', shared assumptions about reality often unknown to the carriers of the assumptions, being subconscious, sometimes suppressed, sometimes so obvious not to be worth verbalizing."

---

[1] While we do commonly look at technology and access to it as a factor helping decide *proxemics,* how do we explain Bronze-Age cities like that of the Indus Valley civilization with their broad intersecting streets designed to allow the prevailing winds to clean them! Or their well-designed cities whose correspondences we only find later in Greek city-states?

In his book *Peace by Peaceful Means: Peace & Conflict, Development and Civilization*, 1996, Prof. Galtung identifies structural violence flowing from cultural violence, and which in turn looks at the *cosmology* of a said group.

The notion of *proxemics* added makes it an interesting aspect where we begin talking of human behaviour in richer nuances in any psycho-cultural analysis of people and groups, including the malevolence of the *anti-culture* including ascertaining their environments that led to a particular adaptation and not another – while we examine their reasons for such differences.

We do find ourselves deal with the interplay of the *proxemics* of any group with their *cultural* cosmology – given the direct relationship between human thought, organization of its spaces & evolution as beings. Where both display a social story, or history that lends particular groups towards particular expressions and developments when compared to others and containing in that social story or history much more than merely what it notes. Or even has been made to note – the moment we compare this set of information with those from other groups/human settlements.

As would be obvious, it raises a set of concerns and queries about how we think about concepts, terms and conceptual tools. Or how to use them like Mark Howard Ross, for example, does in his *The Management of Conflict*, 1993.

We find that we actually are presented with the possibilities of multi-culturalism within academia – where the meaning of *proxemics* involves newer dimensions and dynamics, for example. To the arrival at a certain 'certainty' of human behaviour and its critical dimensions that *proxemics* would mark by itself – while we do grapple with its multi-dimensions that Johan Galtung and/or Mark Howard Ross easily too indicate us towards.

Chapter Five

Change

Always cross-check your
references. Also your intentions.
The best time to take decisions is
when you know all that there is to
be known about a situation.

Always ascertain

What is it?

"As the world starts to move from a primarily vertical – *command and control* – system for creating value to a more horizontal – *connect and collaborate* – value-creation model, and as we blow away more walls, ceilings, and floors at the same time, societies are going to find themselves facing a lot of very profound changes all at once." Or 'the great sorting out' as the Pulitzer Prize winning writer Thomas L Friedman puts it in his book *The World is Flat: The Globalized World in the Twenty-first Century*. That is a 2005 book.

Much earlier in 1970, Alvin Toffler already had spoken of change in different terms. His book *Future Shock* had spoken extensively of change. In different terms than what Thomas L Friedman does in 2005. In fact what Alvin Toffler captures in what causes a *future shock,* in his concept of *accelerative change*, could prove to be a certain critical component to the human world as we see it.

The darker threats

Both the authors differ from what Richard Falk suggests. In a more scholarly work that posits that the future may very well belong to the *terrorist*, aided by the technocrat as well as the traditionalist. Prof. Falk may almost seem prophetic, in his 1987 book *The Promise of World Order: Essays in Normative International Relations*.

But what he suggests have to do with policy-making that is slightly removed from the complex realities of the contemporary world and perhaps seeks easy escapist solutions that never are there – simply because escapist solutions are problems unto themselves. Simplified solutions that are escapist indicate merely to an absence of a comprehension of a problem. They usually occur as reactions to what Alvin Toffler related to as *the pace of accelerative change* when compared to the human capacity for processing and internalization of information – which seems to be a mindboggling pace with globalization thrown in as a comprehensive process.. Or fatigue.

Recent events in West Asia and Europe may seem to bear out Prof. Falk's calamitous warnings, even as Alvin Toffler speaks of societies under tremendous stress because of the pace of change accelerated by human technological prowess that remains far removed from the human capacity for processing and internalizing the sudden minefield of near-endless data that both technology and globalization have brought home. The more dramatic shift has occurred with the multilateralism of the global experience as opposed to the near unilateralism of it that yet marked the colonial periods. We are as much into what Alvin Toffler indicated, and whose one dimension Thomas L Friedman deals in his world *flatteners.* Interesting to note that in a recent study by the World Economic Forum that focuses upon Chinese *globalizers* (corporations from China that have gone global), one comes across an innovative mix of entrepreneurship, innovation and democratic pragmatism borne out of a strategic vision that most successful Chinese *globalizers* display.

Yet the negative aspects of change that Prof. Falk nearly prophesizes possibly can not be a sole outcome of *that* where Deepak Chopra quotes a young Chinese student, in his co-authored book *War of the Worldviews: Science vs Spirituality* with Leonard Mlodinow, who complains that "You ate the whole banquet. Now you give us coffee and dessert, but tell us to pay for the entire meal." In a reference to the behaviour of developed states & societies that Chopra cites as the 'west' – as '*that*' new in-group-out-group formations in the world.

Where is it?

What globalization does via the IT or information technology is what Thomas L. Friedman refers to as the 'flattening' of the world that brings people closer to one another in real time. It does away with the sense of distance, and the blissful ignorance of the assumed esoteric of the new gypsy. Something that the 1980 movie *Blue Lagoon* had captured rather well, while thrusting its actress Brooke Shields to an instant new celebrity status. The unilateral sense of wonder of a diverse world of the new hippie has been replaced by a new enthusiasm of multilateralism, partly shared values and an immense promise of changing individual worlds for the better.

In the new pattern of the connect-and-collaborate model that globalization has introduced, with its IT (Information Technology) aided multilateralism, the promise of changing individual worlds for the better – in a connect-and-collaborate mode Friedman refers to, as one dimension of the postmodern world, as *flattening* is encouraging.

In so far we have been referring to the civil segments of the human world, while we merely have touched upon the uncivil segments and their impacts when we do refer to the recent events in Europe and the US. Yet any analysis of any environment necessarily also enjoins an analysis of the uncivil segments and their impacts – even when camouflaged in civil garbs as the case with many states are. Even when not overtly stated as some are, given that crime is an ubiquitous illness found in most corners of human inhabitation – when not having claimed the entirety of it.

Yet in the predominant civil segments, the impact of globalization riding information and other technologies is lending us towards a different mode of interactions than could be thought about a century ago. Clearly we are in a new age. From the largely A-Line command and control structure of the modern *nation-state*. In the view of Friedman, this flattening of the world helps build bridges; and I happily suspect, the *global citizen* as well.

Even if this motor of the postmodern is shared, as Friedman correctly notes, by everyone who can, and it is no longer the prerogative of the tourist industry in banana republics. Fast bringing down old privileges and prejudices as well, it also engineers a new diffidence amongst groups & increasingly individuals that feel threatened by an overwhelming pace. Or worse, by an alien culture they can neither identify nor put their fingers to it except as some ubiquitous 'west' and 'modernity'.

Ironically, finally sharing in bits and pieces with the developed societies and states their sense of *future shock* that Alvin Toffler had so elucidated. Adding to the *future shock* in manners not anticipated by Toffler, the recent events in West Asia and Europe (and to some extent within the United States, where a two-term Presidency by a Nobel Prize winning President of half-African origins has brought some domestic churns within a society that already was suffering from Toffler's *future shock*; and the strains of what Paul Kennedy already had noted in 1998 about its various forays into global military exercises – *the imperial overstretch*) merely help bring forth Prof. Richard Falk's observations as somewhat prophetic.

It is facile to confuse the uncivil with the new emergent multilateralism. Or overlook the participation of the uncivil as the newer actor in global politics as a formal *fait accompli*. As the dirty sewer, colonialism is taking off some of the covers off itself in areas where they did not get flushed out with history that Friedman's *flat world* envisages. They too form part of the world. Now check some of the following diagrams. Each broadly signifies an organizational type and you can often give yours a mix – depending upon which functions best in your case.

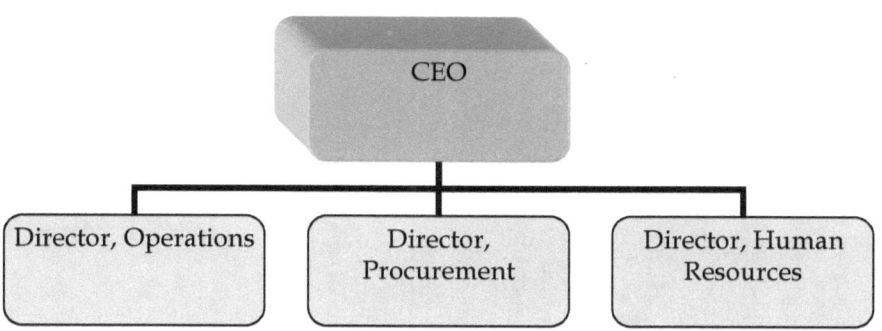

1. *A typical A-Line authority model.*

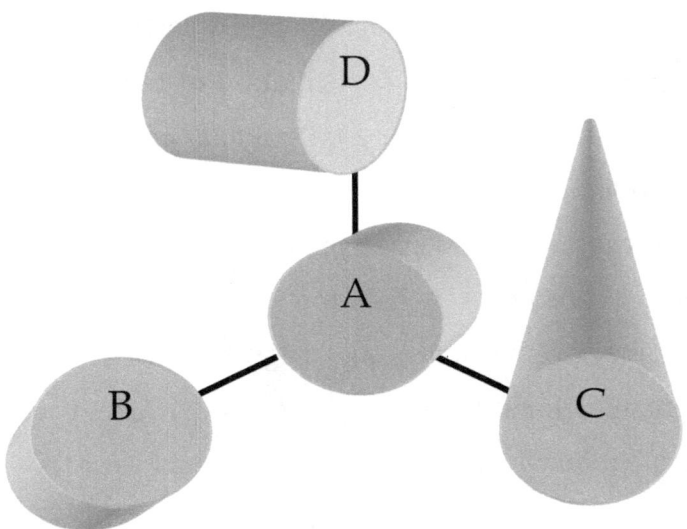

2. *A typical connect-collaborate model.*

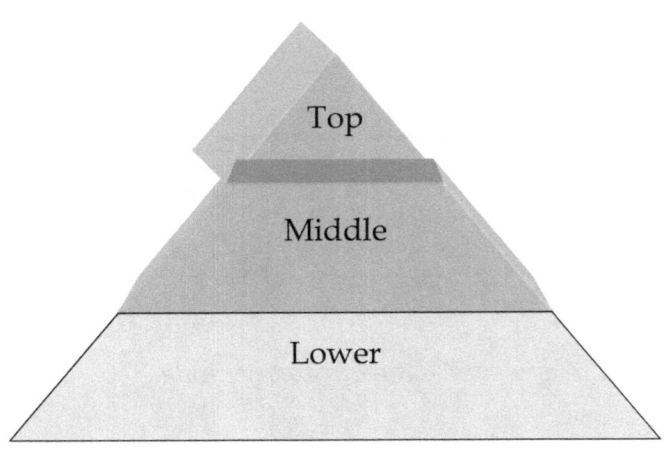

3. *A-Line collaborative model of hierarchies.*

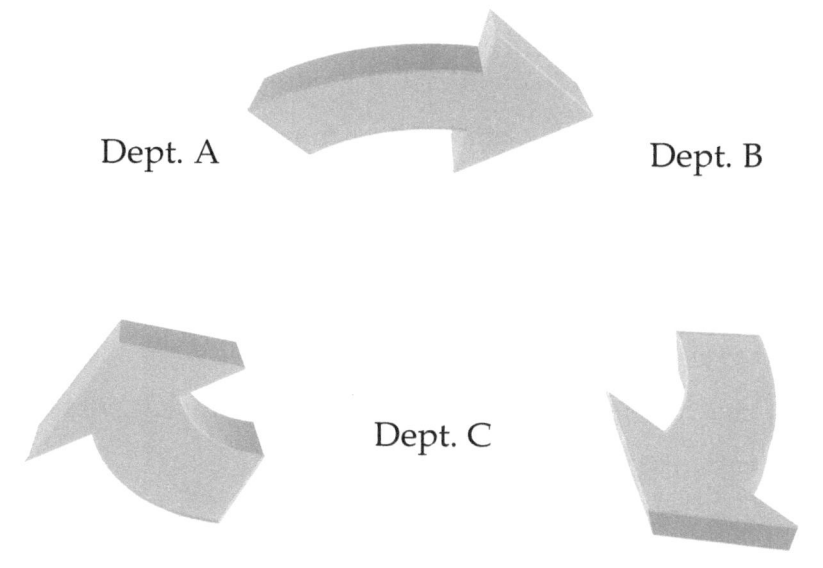

Dept. A

Dept. B

Dept. C

4. A horizontal collaborative organizational model.

Each of the models signifies a broad type. Thus from the modern A-Line hierarchy models of command & control (command & control lines delineate the organizational structure as well as mark the delegation process within any organization, and obviously occur during/after staffing), to the horizontal collaborative model (you can easily replace departments with individuals in the diagram given. Or even in any diagram to suit your organizational attributes), each of the organizational structure also indicate a different approach to management. Keep that in your mind. Choosing an organizational structure is a critical task and your approach to management gets reflected there – of all things.

You can easily envisage if a typical A-Line structure suits your needs or a more *avant garde* horizontal collaborative model suits your needs. We have shown just four of the various types here. In fact you can mix and match models based upon your requirements. Innovation & flexibility is the key.

In the next chapter we are going to take a look at crime-terror. It is useful to have a comprehension of what the topics mean, apart the news reports of devastating impacts. Are they part of your environment?

Things to do:

1. Which basic type of organizational model do you prefer? Why?

2. What are the particular "embedded" management approaches/styles you can think of that come with the four basic types shown here?

3. How far do you think improved technology in terms of transport, telecommunications, banking functions, etc. can help you opt for a different organizational structure than what you would prefer at the moment?

4. How far do you think finding the correct Human Resources to fill in the requirements matter? Are they critical to your organization's functioning?

Chapter Six

Terrorism: Should One Worry?

What is terrorism?

Nothing could be more unsettling for any business and living than incidents of crime and terror. Apart the violence, are they a regular feature of your environment? Both can be part of your ordinary life without making it to news reports that get the UNO's attention. In fact when we do look at the various locales around the globe, we do distinctly mark different places differently. Do we not? A Peshawar or Kandahar in Afghanistan, or a Mosul in Iraq mean different things than a Singapore in SE Asia or a Hong Kong SAR in China. Or a Rio de Janeiro in Brazil or a Stockholm in Sweden. It is what we call *the quality of life* in those places. How is it in your area?

It is useful to first begin with a description of the topic at hand. Many often do end up asking, *"What is Terrorism?"* You would be surprised to know that the commonsensical answer that "terrorism is that what *terrorizes",* is also what scholarly answers point at. But *what* terrorizes *whom*? is equally important a question & *how?* As we read further, we will find that the answers, however, in scholastic terms seem quite complex and often sophisticated. This is because of the concerns of scholars about the various moral theories and concerns involved with the topic of *violence.* Included in those concerns are also concerns about the Human Rights of those who *terrorize.* Even if such concerns may seem the furthest removed from the concerns of those who do so, i.e. *terrorize*!

Simplifying terrorism is good business sense

Contrary to what it may seem to scholars, simplifying terrorism is good business sense. This is because it includes crime as well and they do form the two scourges both business & living can do well to identify and avoid. In brief, it is quite accurate to consider as *terroristic* those acts that *terrorize*—given the functional attribute of *terrorism* as an act where it seeks to *terrorize*. This may involve direct and/or indirect violence; or threats of violence. We usually use technical classifications to refer to mediated direct violence that is organized, and both terrorism and crime seem to meet that.

This helps, as you will see, achieve two seemingly divergent objectives. One, we can easily club crime & terrorism together. Second, by making a distinction between crime and terrorism, states and governments find it functionally easier to operate and deal with the two scourges.

> What to do if crime seems the dominant mode and value-driver in your area? Look for other areas that are different.

Imponderables?

Across contemporary Terrorism

Transnational terrorism, like transnational crime, presents the problem of verification. This is because they do not operate openly like the registered corporate houses, with a public audit of its activities and finances. In the face of the difficulties of verification, it is useful to look at the various processes of change that are at play. This helps us to identify the particular challenges of transnational terrorism, and its relative success. The challenge is to identify *permissive* causes within states and locate the *proximate* causes that transnational terrorism exploits.

The transnational nature of contemporary terrorism also presents another kind of analytical problem not captured by traditional security frameworks, although transnational terrorism is said to have been *securitized* after 11 September 2001. Simply because information technology has made the erstwhile idea of the free radicals suddenly come home – in its amorphous net-workings.

Traditional security frameworks, even the expanded version by Buzan *et al*, are concerned with states where security threats are seen from a state or a group of states, to another state or group of states. This statist perspective is natural to the sub-discipline of *Security Studies* within *International Relations.*

Yet, terrorism is a threat that is direct to any state and its civilian populace – when it is not crime alone as the punishment for being alive, for its populace. It can be from within, or home-grown. Or it can be from outside the state's boundaries. It is here that the ambiguity makes it much more an insidious threat to any state – given the possibility of *terrorism* used as state-craft: by one state against another state.

Terrorism globalized

The transnational nature of the kind of terrorism that the Al-Qaeda (as an example) represents is unique in its organization and functioning. But even in that, newer versions (ISIS) have emerged and have helped bring the topic under a fresh scrutiny. The usage of apparent free radicals, as the ISIS shows in its alleged recent European operations, make this a different kind of threat within the context of a globalized world, with the European territory forming the *home* for its terrorists and not some remote Afghan hill or a West Asian desert town or the bushes of Maghreb Africa. It may rightly be called post-modern terrorism, even as it is rabidly *anti-modern*.

It is a security threat from a non-state entity dispersed far and wide geographically and where its rationale escapes one – though continuing to be apparently religious and/or ideological. Their impacts upon the average business environment are of introducing a new unsavoury uncertainty at a societal level.

The threat that it presents to states is direct and particularly insidious, owing to its leaderless organization that consists of phantom cells, networked globally in a digitally integrated world. Its second danger arises from its riding on the wave of religious fanaticism currently sweeping the world, and inviting disparate elements in its rabid war against the liberal democratic world.

The difference between international, multinational, and transnational lies in the location of the main body or bodies. Transnational indicates an absence of any particular location whose destruction may also destroy the entire entity. This new face of *transnational terrorism* as opposed to merely a multi-national one indicates a widely dispersed cellular organization that is amorphous, and where disruption does not necessarily mean destruction of the organization. Something that though difficult is yet possible to achieve with multi-national crime-terror groups.

To get at transnational terrorism analytically, necessarily, involves studying the processes that make its existence(s) possible. We thus include culture *via* religion as an important variable. This means introducing the study of psycho-cultural factors at work, within any given process at work and play. In other words, studying transnational terrorism too is the study of a global phenomenon! The factors at work are many, and the approach needs to be *transdisciplinary*, i.e. eclectic.

But why are we studying about crime-terror in EA? You may ask. Simply because we are dealing with the environment that also has these players and who often do function as ordinary business/humanitarian interests before one discovers their colours!

Analysis & re-thinking

As Johan Galtung has pointed out, any analysis or understanding of conflicts necessitates an understanding of the *deep culture* or *cosmology.* Moreover, wherever any terrorist organization is not a state-sponsored one, its functioning and operational costs involve certain processes. This is where crime co-habits with terrorism more fluidly.

The fact that technical definitions of terrorism point at incidents of direct violence, often help obscure the topicality of the subject. Such incidents are known as *events* and occur within certain *processes* that underlie it.

This is true of all events in the human world, as well as the natural one. Studying the process(es) then, is a crucial factor since terror acts do not occur round-the-clock at any given location. They occur in sudden bursts, where the period between two *events* remains as crucial as the first *event* itself. However, if any strategic shift in how people think and imagine is to be terrorism's objective, it is forerun by crime.

Crime and compliance involve necessary socialization patterns and forces that mean the diabolical as opposed to that of Human Rights, individual freedom and an environment free from coercion and/or fear that the state's orderliness promises and enters a contract into - for. Overtaking and overthrowing the psycho-dynamics of the state by crime mean the obvious. Thus places & people that show a pre-dominance of crime over the state also indicate a lengthy process of failures & appropriations: a strong negative in EA since socialization processes exhibiting societal value-systems are critical here.

Groups of developed democratic states like those that form the European Union & North-west Europe, Canada & the USA; and the group of developing/transitional democracies like India mark for interesting comparative studies. This is because of the various dynamics at play, including the commonality of an *interactive-embeddedness* in a globalized world.

> Networking is crucial for civil societies. Any preponderance of crime-terror means a stressed civil society.

If they can, so can you!

The case of weak states

Transitional states like India have their internal conflicts also said to have acquired transnational characteristics, amidst a growing religious | ideological fundamentalism in Indian society and general break down of an already severely stretched state-machinery. The double bind is where any Human Rights parameter clubbed with the socialization processes that are at work, and play, posits much of the Indian state as crime-terror. But then who are they?

This has to do more with the basic composition of such transitional states that are medieval at their best, or pre-social at most parts. Finding in such states the ripe breeding | feeding grounds of rabid *anti-modernism* qua anti-west almost seem natural. The crops are what turn up as unpalatable crime-terror. Thus making the study of the socialization processes and elite-manipulations more critical topics, within the study of terrorism and which necessarily include the psycho-cultural dynamics behind them.

Interactive-embeddedness

The *interactive-embeddedness*, within a globalized world involves a necessary study of the presences of the developed democracies in such flailing ones. One needs to look at their interactions and their various modes, including their inputs in the socialization processes, and elite-manipulations.

Especially where the uncivil segments seek to ambush and hijack those. Or especially where the political-state frameworks do present the uncivil by themselves! Since contemporary transnational terrorism is anti-modern, a meaningful understanding of the phenomenon necessitates understanding that what constitutes *anti-modern*. An *eclectic* approach thus becomes imperative for the topic at hand. Given the particular peculiar nature of South Asian transitional democracies like India and Pakistan, their nuclear statuses do not make them more stable as states or societies. But merely magnify the threats in horrific manners in apocalyptic scenarios.

The inherent unstable nature of their societies, and the various ills that stem from their socialization processes/elite manipulations, render the kind of transitional democracies like the South Asian ones as ripe cases for transnational crime-terrorism to breed in & feed upon. A strategic threat to the rest of the developed democratic world, this also jeopardizes the environment.

> Always take a bird-eye's view of places and countries. The cumulative picture is a more accurate one than bits and pieces.

Get complete pictures

Checking differences

China, as a single-party democracy power in the Asian region however does not present that spectre of nightmares in apocalyptic scenarios. It actually comes across, even if as a potent strategic threat of the megalomaniac for some in its region[2], as a minimizing factor for such possibilities of any apocalyptic scenarios that terrorism, transitional poor democracies & nuclear weapons or WMD (weapons for mass destruction) present, when put together in a mixing jar.

The problem is made more acute by the largely illiterate, medieval peasantry-based populaces of the sub-continent that also are prone to bouts of fabulous & rabid anti-modernisms. Even if not exhibiting it as uniformly as their cultivators would have liked to imagine them as exhibition pieces, or as directly. Their multi-party democratic system (read liberal in India while Islamic in Pakistan), assuming to function as one, within such constituencies, do indeed present peculiar challenges of their own! This occurs from a contradiction their structural imperatives present viz their societal ones. This then presents one with the usual explanations of the colonial period and the post-colonial emergence from or re-engagement with it.

---

[2] The idea of authoritarian states like China turning megalomaniac or tyrannical in its external relations is a fear some ASEAN states do share in private. The other end of the spectrum easily include flailing and weak states with a dysfunctional system and where individuals, as well as a criminal take-over of the state presents one with the same scenario – merely mitigated in the corruption payoffs that when made eliminate the threat; when not turn it as diabolic as the mafiosi's extortions even if all accruing via state-actors. India presents a spectre of the other end of the spectrum in the region.

Despite the usual arguments of the impact of colonialism to have introduced modernity in pre-modern societies and/or groups, their failures to adapt and of socialization introduces a certain morbidity in the human condition, creating fissures and a corrosive humanity in many situations. This turns identity into a ready and emotive topic that also is cultivated as a reactive phenomenon rather than a proactive one, and often in the negative sense of the word *reaction*. Yet comparisons with the developed democracies and the roles of them within such regions mark for interesting notations & viewpoints.

Things to do:

1. Do you see anything that has changed for the better in your area?
2. Do you see anything that has changed for the worse in your area?
3. Do you know any senior citizens who may help you record a few more of the two kinds of changes? If yes, have you noted them down?
4. How would you rate your area with a. the nearest larger city? b. With the nearest city in your region? c. The largest city in your country? d. Your dream city in the entire globe?
5. What do you think can be done to improve your area when compared with the above?
6. What do you think is possible to do to improve, i.e. can be done to improve your area when compared with other areas?
7. Compare the reasons behind the differences. What do you think?

Chapter Seven
Dealing with Change of all kinds

15 EASY Steps to Combating Terrorism-Crime Internal security paradigms:

State-Civil Society co-operation

1. WHY does my neighbourhood policeman/policewoman seem like a..... CRIMINAL?
2. Report Crime – Any crime. Even small ones.
3. Report any delay or discouragement or coercive behaviour from the police or officials when you report a crime.
4. Form your own Citizen Vigilance Committees/Clubs/etc. that promote democracy while discouraging crime & criminals.
5. Follow the Club Shopping example.
6. Club Shopping is a concept where ordinary business & citizens interact. They make shopping/business a membership oriented venture where criminals, etc. are not allowed or actively discouraged from membership.
7. **Encourage the network growth of membership of such Club Shopping.**
8. Who are CRIMINALS?

   A criminal would be a person who:

   a. actively commits criminal acts and/or encourages crime and criminal behaviour.
   b. passive actor in criminal acts and encourages indirect criminal acts via wilful ignorance (law enforcement officials, people in positions of power, etc.) or refuses to take your complaints seriously against other offenders.
   c. People who encourage an environment of fear and coercion to affect your average normal expectation of **free-**

from-fear democratic life & individual freedom.

9. Encourage the growth of networked societies in similar areas like Human Rights, Citizens' Forums, etc. while actively filtering membership for criminals.

10. Discourage the inclusion of criminals in your networked societies – like Club Shopping, etc. You can easily form communities that discourage crime while encouraging individual freedom and material growth. Keep weeding your own networked societies for 'home-grown' crime/criminal tendencies. It is amazing how much of delinquency can be home-grown.

11. Form your Citizen's Forums, etc. that has active access to your local/regional/national representative(s). Have them participate actively in your concerns.

12. Be careful whom you give your vote to. Discourage criminals from entering public life via elections, etc.

13. Demand a 100% transparency public file on each candidate that seeks to enter the public life.

14. Demand a 100% transparency file on each official that already exist. You can begin with your local law-enforcement/government officials/police stations, etc. Make them accountable to the Citizens' Forum.

15. Make yourself accountable to government/local/etc. authorities.

Now with the above 15 steps, we now also know how to secure ourselves against crime, criminals & terrorists (to a large extent) without jeopardizing our freedoms. It is useful if we also do take a look at the various issues that present themselves – for all effective purposes – to us.

In the next chapter, we are going to take a quick look at some critical concerns that fuel disputes and conflicts that we read about as terrorist acts. They usually deal with identity issues while common crime largely deals with the issue of lazy boors that seek to rob (using violence or the threat of violence) to gain material wealth and with usual complete disregard of human welfare & respect for life.

Or even any common marker that we employ for a civic life in human society that the state-system marks for most. We aren't looking at societies/states taken over by criminals as the issue of corruption often throws up. It is interesting to note that petty crime & criminals often occur at the substratum of terror as well. Yet in the sudden maze of reports of violence that we often ascribe to religion etc. – identity and identity-politics are an issue. Yet if looked at carefully, we find that most protagonists are unable to actually defend their ideas of religion and religiosity outside the private sphere that it is marked as – as a personal matter and which includes the right to non-faith. In other words, religious terrorism is a failure within that religion first. Before it seeks to make a public statement of it via terror.

When we lend a little of thought and introspection to the real issues within identity and identity-politics, we find what we encounter in the next chapter as the key topics, outside the maelstrom of personal failures, idiosyncrasies and blatant ignorance that rule the world of crime. As that of terror, we find that we already have dealt with their failures unless state failures accrue for worse violence and atrocity that then encourage a reaction as crime-terror. The two instances are distinct and different.

Chapter Eight

The Clash of Claims & Opinions

We find that business and living both seek conditions of peace, orderliness and prosperity. Yet, they demand a socialization that supports that. We commonly have identified Human Rights help do this. Yet apart individual failures and human depravity, we seem to be further removed from what most recognize and seek. How is it so? Human history consists of and is made up of the principles of ideal life having been found, or claimed to have been found. The ironical clash of claims over who is more correct usually comes much later.

"You mean you took the entire sack for yourself while promoting selflessness?"

Much later when one finds most humans have suitably become the prisoners of their own discursive creations, and what they term as their inventions – both mechanical as well as *reified* notions and ideas (like state and society) that form the structure. Someone bundling those ages of celebrations of 'prisonership' into books that go famously by the name of Clash of Civilizations isn't too surprising. Prof. Samuel P. Huntington's work remains an important work that has touched upon a few things. The more beautiful part is that it may be more correctly termed as "The Clash of Claims & Opinions." That it all boils down to history (as lost human lives and opportunities while plundering the earth though) is what escapes most of the sensible portions of humanity.

So getting back to the central issues in academia, which in turn, deals with the central issues of human life, I do think that the two following issues are and form the building blocks of the Human cognitive world:

1. The notion of identity or the question: *Who Am I?*

2. The notion of gender or the questions: *What does it mean to be a man and a woman, respectively?*

Many often wonder if such profound questions visit the majority of people. They actually do. In myriad forms and manners. While one does have scarcity as a first cause of human depravity – human development would posit some judicious

How is it?

Marking the unsavoury rotundity of a globalized world, in its uncivil parts that are riding the same flattening principle of Thomas L Friedman – but as the free radicals & groups in what is fast emerging as Europe's new nightmare is a concern that one necessarily needs to take care of in today's business.

> The forces of chaos & disorder are often few. Hence their noises & violence the more loud…the more desperate!

Always examine disappointments twice over, if you should examine your success only once.

One suspects also of the many developing and fragile states – the new globalization of the uncivil segments, often in newer imaginary ties as opposed to the real ones that mark Friedman's *flat world* including their rationales. Although the global economy of these uncivil segments that mark the grey-market, in their assumed linkages and rationales, as well as products of fractitious as well as misplaced elite-manipulations – those remain common in their shared incivilities as state-societal attributes; and of a sizeable amount and economy as well. Thus from there too emerges the various (often violent) thoughts and views seeking to change the very many aspects and attributes they read more facilely as a colonial product, than a Friedman's *flat world*.

Revisionism is not a new undercurrent, and China is largely pragmatic and well-placed to usher in the *intelligent actor* as a major world power. Many harbouring revisionism often assume and/or imagine to piggyback ride differences for their own corrective measures & retributions. Similar to how they would manipulate any faultline to suit their objectives. Often enjoined as a alarming concept within geo-politics, revisionism management techniques as its ready anti-dote. So why would we seem to fail so consistently while having so successfully colonized the planet? It is easier, it may seem, to fight and kill than to live and share. But then to return to the second of the twin questions: once when one has answered the second question – within the context of the nature of the Clash of Claims & Opinions, *"What should it mean to be a woman and a man, respectively?"* One does find that the imaginations of the answers to these two questions do form the crux of the problems in human lives. Answering them correctly? Well.....? You got it!

Most great contributions to human life and academia are considered to be those that have contributed to The Clash of Claims & Opinions. Though not very intelligent, I still believe myself to be democratic to the best of my abilities and hence would not and do not want to contribute to *The Clash of Claims & Opinions*. My belief urges me that in case of differences of opinions, one usually can beg to differ, or agree to agree, or disagree without any participant causing any injury to anyone – to the best degree possible, excluding one's disappointment over a few things. I would be disappointed if my friends disagree with me and would yet go out and share an evening with them. I mean those kinds of disappointments that are assumed to be civilized, without putting the term civilization into disrepute.

Some say that the notion of culture is what makes a civilization in the long run. Very precious those times then – that allows culture to develop and civilizations to be made. Although as most sensible people would agree, both the term *culture* and *civilization* forego of any conditions of direct violence and avoid any condition of indirect violence! That is why I do think that Prof. Samuel P. Huntington's book *The Clash of Civilizations & the re-making of World Orders* – given the wide uninformed heat and discussion it can and has generated – should have been more apt as *The Clash of Claims & Opinions!* In ability & wisdom, as a particular life form that is of the earth and dependent upon the earth!

Now having read a little about what really gets the goat of many people who continue blaming religion or ideology for their personal failures, it is useful to have a first-hand idea of what really good states (welfare states) are all about. Together it helps us get a fair idea of the various expectations amidst failures, if any, before we decide upon a place as our investment destination. We shall later deal with how we actually can help effect positive changes in places that we have chosen, amidst the range the globe presents to us. But right now, in the next chapter we will study a little about welfare states first.

Things to do:

1. How do people solve differences between friends and strangers in your area?

2. How would you prefer they be done?

3. Do you think violence is an answer? When and why would you think violence is an answer, if you do?

4. Are you aware of discussions and debates?

5. Are people aware of the two in your area?

6. What are the modalities for them?

7. Does the environment in your area encourages violence or encourages peaceful methods of conflict resolution?

8. How would you rate the public utilities of your area when compared to your favourite village, town and/or city?

Chapter Nine

Welfare States

The idea of the Welfare State is something beautiful. Every democracy is a welfare state. The difference lies in the degree. One hopes that so far, it is good enough! A welfare state simply means a state whose paramount interest lies in the welfare of its citizens. Of course that there then can be other kinds of states defeats one's imaginations! But there are while there also are the welfare states!

Let us look at the Nordic States. The beautiful part is that the state-civil society relationship there are not antagonistic. Now let us look at the more liberal states- the UK, the USA, etc. and one does find a certain antagonistic relationship between the state and civil society. The academia usually becomes a good marker for such states in listing their expressions that exhibit a state-civil society relationship that is antagonistic or not. That is, however, not to confuse differences and freedom of expression found as evidences for an antagonistic state-civil society.

The notion of a welfare state is in the recognition that the state exists for its people. Not people for the state. Given the basis of welfare states (the rationale that explains state-civil society relations), the idea behind encouraging Welfare States has to take into account a few things: *The idea of the state as well as that of citizenship.* Given the notion of the Welfare State, like the Nordic states - the encouragement of Welfare states have to necessarily take into account *the state-civil society relationship and what accrue behind such differences.*

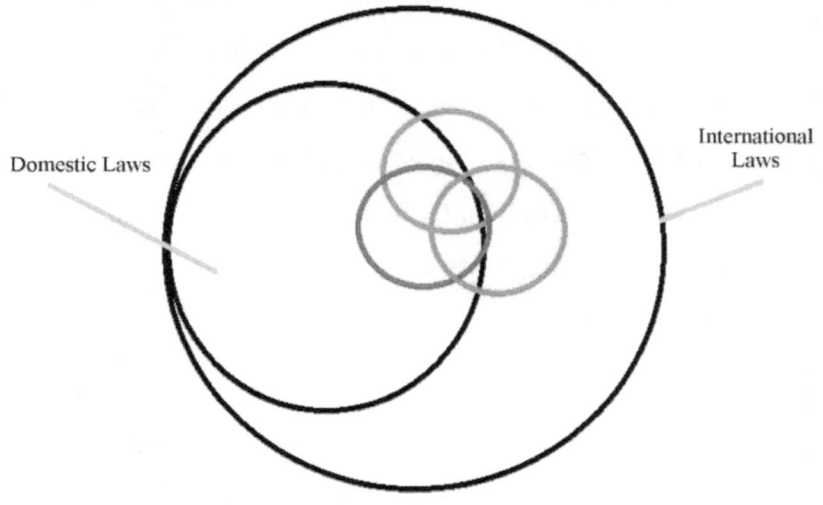

Domestic Laws

International Laws

The P= perceiving agent, O= an observed other, X= a third phenomenal object model bound within the larger set of law where domestic laws form a sub-set within intl. Covenants & laws. Eg. Universal Declaration of Human Rights.

The positive triad: State-civil society-law

A study into those differences is what one would be looking at before one promotes the notion of a welfare state. Third World states that can be considered to be in the transitional mode (still in the momentum of state/nation building), the opportunity is much more in being able to encourage its movement towards the idea of the Welfare State, on the lines of the Nordic states.

The tough part lies in first educating the state and the populace over the meanings of being a citizen and being a part of the state. The fundamental notion of being liberal democratic that can enthuse and generate enough of social capital to become a Welfare State! My previous writings do speak about such needs with respect to state-nation building. It is less about statistics and more about what begets those statistics, even as one recognizes the bikini-nature of statistics in social sciences!

In other words, before one advocates the Welfare state, one has to be very clear about the meanings of the state and citizenship as well as state/nation building! As usually become the case in many fragile states, the tough parts usually do not get answered and one has writings like these to mention those devilish necessities! When they do not, then it does become the case of putting the cart in front of the horse, with the horse standing about fifteen metres behind!

In that proverbial fifteen metres, are the differences of the Nordic States and the notion of socialism as some communitarian excursion minus a community (more critically, minus the community-feeling and which isn't the mafiosi-tended sense of belonging in case failed politicians from weak/flailing states also read this). It is not necessarily communitarian, though the Nordic model does become a future tense for liberal democracies - with the assumed degree of alienation being the lowest!

Ideally speaking of course as academia is wont to. Including the difference between developing states, nationalism versus developed states, and patriotism! The notion of the Welfare state is irrevocably a democratic one, should one be referring to the Nordic model. The encouragement of the uncivil society (crime-terror-prostitution) is not the Welfare state model! It is simply the uncivil society. Not socialism.

Things to do:
1. What do you understand by welfare?
2. Is there someone in your family availing welfare? Is it enough to ensure a human life with dignity?
3. What do you understand by taxation? Do you pay taxes? Why?
4. What do you understand how prices for products are set? Do you know how prices are set for perishable goods like vegetables, meat, fish and eggs?
5. Do you know how prices are set for durable consumer goods like electric kettle, electric iron, refrigerator, etc.?
6. How much do you on an average spend on paying taxes (including indirect ones that are levied through the purchase of goods) in a month?
7. Are you satisfied with the civic returns that you get from the state for your taxes?

8. What do think the word *state* means? What do you think the word *civil-society* means?

9. Have you thought about the various areas where the two intersect and actually help make life better?

10. How does one strengthen basic *state-civil society* interstices and areas they often overlap?

11. In the preceding diagram, if the two of the over-lapping circles are the *state* & *civil society*, do you think the third is the constitutional guarantee and definitions the two are defined, described and circumscribed by?

Chapter Ten

Deriving our action-plans

Having seen the A-Line organizational structure, it is often easy to assume that the POSDCORB logic works best there. However, it is not necessarily true and one may adapt to one's needs and abilities. The moment we do speak of organizations, we also necessarily are speaking about management approaches/styles as well.

The modern A-Line organizational structure works best where regular exchange and interactions take place amongst employees/workers that require regular monitoring and captive attention, or the *principle of exclusivity* that many organizations often emphasize upon. This simply means that any employee will work exclusively for the organization and not lend or sell his/her skills outside the organization. Usually such *exclusivity principles* that demand employee-captivity is common in A-Line organizations and often pay a better compensation package for the contractual period.

Many often seek a sense of permanence and prefer these kinds of organizational requirements to the relative freedom that post-modern models like the connect-collaborate models allow. The various kinds of employee preferences vary from economy to economy; and place to place. This usually has a whole load of factors including development levels, literacy and the penetration of technology and globalization. Post-modern models like the connect-collaborate models allow for a much greater degree of personal as well as professional freedom. They usually are adopted by younger professionals with a larger degree of mobility and high professional performances/ethics. Instead of any authority line, connect-collaborate models allow for greater creativity as well and often include the outsourcing market to a larger degree. It however relies upon the higher professional ethics to survive and is a preferred mode for most professionals who seek independence.

Thinking about it

Now let us take a quick look at how data is generated, given our widespread reliance (and correctly so) upon data for forming our opinions or drawing our inferences.. The more common model about our world is the chain-model (string theory) even as many posit the idea of some chaos theory in the complications of physical and mathematical tabulations & calculations.

The figure in the next page would remind you about the example of connect-collaborate model that we saw earlier. The diagram remains the same here, except that the parameters have changed – thus changing the meaning of it. Interesting, is it not? This also helps us note the heuristic nature – the usage of models as tools to speak variously! Like we do with concepts. They too are tools that we use to communicate an idea better! It is crucial that we take a realistic view of the human knowledge systems that include our educational processes, etc. as tools. That is what they were designed as. The figure below talks of three basic crucial features of the human world. 1. Human Cognitive Universes (note the plural form). 2. The Natural physical universe (note the singular form despite the plural nature of it quantum physics emphasizes). 3. Inventions, Technology and Adaptation that occur when we face the natural physical world.

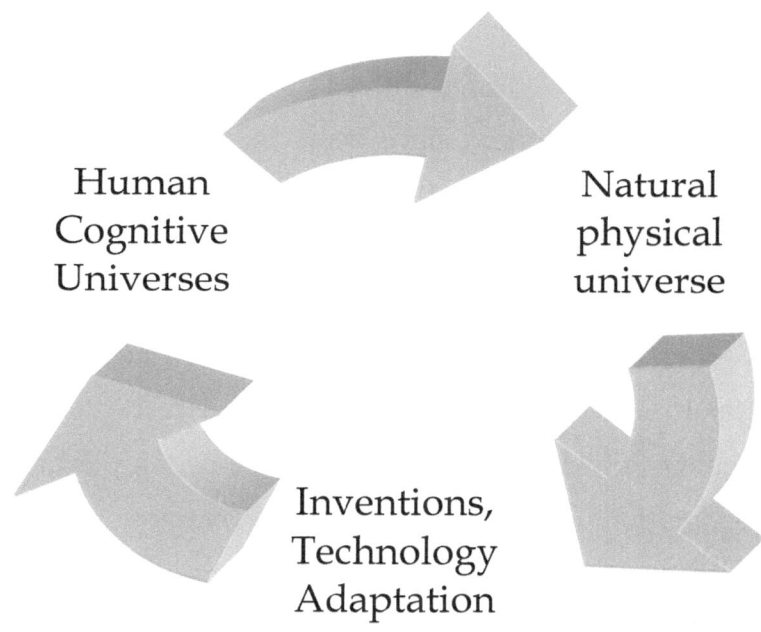

Human
Cognitive
Universes

Natural
physical
universe

Inventions,
Technology
Adaptation

The basic knowledge-building model.

As is evident, the three basic features mentioned before display the synergy that orders the human universes. This is simply because humans continue being the single known planetary life-form that invents complex artificial technology and its various adaptations. This it evidently does when it faces the physical natural world. Human adaptations via technology and inventions have an impact about how humans have come to view life and living itself.

We frankly would not have been discussing EA, if that would not have been the case. In fact so complete has been the human colonization of the planetary surface that many forget that we are creatures upon planet earth that are dependent upon its surface air, water and life-forms for our basic survival and sustenance. In other words, the human world of artifice has nearly taken over many human cognitive universes even as human adaptations like technology & Inventions have an understandable impact upon human imaginations.

That they do have the unintended impacts (largely) upon the natural physical world is what perilous situations (largely human-made) and their comprehensions mark much for. The recent summit in 2016, in a human made settlement called Paris over the global climate change merely helps serve the point better, following as it did closely behind the incidents of violence in the same city.

Research methodologies simply refer to the methodology used to gather data. Usually they broadly conform to the 1. *Quantitative method.* 2. *The Qualitative method.* Both of them also refer to approaches and theories in philosophy as well as the natural sciences. Quantitative methodology focuses more upon numbers or figures to mean data that usually is mathematical. Simply put: If two women purchase five bottles of perfumes each, what does it tell us?

Needless to say the above question can be read as an easy question although it is not. While we know that two women purchased five bottles of perfumes each, the data is interesting in its range: 1. 10 bottles of perfume were sold (seller). 2 10 bottles of perfume were bought (consumer). We can see that both the categories span a further set of queries depending upon what we wish to know and for what *purpose.* This is simple quantitative methodology.

A qualitative methodology would have further sets of queries that would seek to know 1. Who were the two women? 2. Why were the five bottles of perfume purchased? This we can see provides us with a greater detail than the first approach and is often employed more in the social sciences that deal with learning about/comprehending human behaviour.

Of the two basic approaches, we would also need to look at how the data is collected. The first is simpler and can easily be had from the seller's counter. The second approach that seeks to unearth greater details that may involve personal choice and decisions/preferences are a little more difficult to come by. One has to be clear that research methodologies are unobtrusive fact finding exercises that aren't interrogations in legal custody. How we seek to elicit those responses and facts are determined obviously by our purpose as well as the manner of going about it.

Going about the manner of it is research methodology. Going about the purpose is plain academic research that entails sufficient prior study within a subject to arrive at a topic. Given the two basic approaches that we see here that delineate research methodologies, we also can see that they actually are very limited exercises in their scope and range unless specifically designed for a particular purpose. Commoner methods of data collection include questionnaires, response-games that involve volunteer participants, observations, etc.

Things to do:

1. Type out a set of questions that you would like people on the streets to answer. Given the time each would ordinarily be able to squeeze out, what kind of answers would you expect?
2. If you would have people tick the correct answers, what kind of range would you be providing them in the questionnaire that best suits your purpose?
3. How would you rate the shift in opinions over a period of time?
4. If you do have to conduct a survey (that is what it is), do you think the topic will dictate whether your approach is a quantitative one or a qualitative one?
5. What are the possible differences that occur to you in the kinds of questionnaires you would be designing when designing a questionnaire that asks about 1. A product (shampoo/perfume/cigarettes/etc.). 2. Opinions (what do they think about an issue: Human Rights/Law & Order/Civic amenities/etc.)?

Selected References

Alex Schmid and Albert J. Jongman, *Political Terrorism* (New Brunswick: Transaction Books, 1988).

Alexander Wendt, *Social Theory of International Politics* (Cambridge: Cambridge University Press, 1999).

Alvin Toffler, *Future Shock* (New York: Random House, 1970).

Ashish Nandy, ed., *Science, Hegemony and Violence* (New Delhi: Oxford University Press, 1988).

Ashustosh Varshney, *Ethnic Conflict and Civic Life: Hindus and Muslims in India* (New Delhi: Oxford University Press, 2002)

Barry Buzan, *People, States, and Fear: The National Security Problem in International Relations* (New Delhi: Transasia Publishers, 1987).

Barry Buzan, et al, *Security: A New Framework For Analysis* (Boulder, Colorado: Lynne Rienner Publishers, 1998).

Benjamin R. Barber, *Jihad vs. McWorld: Terrorism's Challenge to Democracy (New York: Ballantine Books, 2001 Edition).*

Bruce Hoffman, *Inside Terrorism* (New York: Columbia University Press, 1998).

Bruce B. Campbell and Arthur D. Brenner, eds. *Death Squads in Global Perspective: Murder with Deniability* (Hampshire: Macmillan Press Ltd., 2000).

Charles Funderburk & Robert G. Thobaben, *Political Ideologies: Left, Center, Right* (New York: HarperCollins College Publishers, Inc., 1994).

Chris Brown, *International Relations Theory: New Normative Approaches* (New York: Columbia University Press, 1992).

David Campbell & Michael Dillon, eds. *The Political Subject of Violence* (Manchester: Manchester University Press, 1993).

David Held, *Political Theory and the Modern State* (New Delhi: Maya Polity, 1998), Indian reprint.

David J. Whittaker, ed., *The Terrorism Reader* (London: Routledge, 2001).

David J. Whittaker, *Terrorism: Understanding the Global Threat* (London: Pearson Education Ltd., 2002).

Deepak Chopra & Leonard Mlodinow, *War of the Worldviews: Science vs Spirituality* (London: Rider, 2011).

Detter De Lupis, *The Law of War* (Cambridge: Cambridge University Press, 1987).

Edward W. Said, *Orientalism* (New York: Pantheon Books, 1977).

Edward W. Said, *Culture and Imperialism* (New York: Alfred A. Knopf, 1993).

F.S. Northedge, *The International Political System* (London: Faber & Faber, 1976).

Feliks Gross, *Violence in Politics* (The Hague: Mouton & Co., NV., 1972).

G.B. Madison, *The Political Economy of Civil Society and Human Rights* (London: Routledge, 1998).

Howard Davis, ed., *Ethics and Defence: Power and Responsibility in the Nuclear Age* (Oxford: Basil Blackwell Ltd., 1986).

James F. Hoge, Jr., and Fareed Zakaria, eds. *The American Encounter: The United States and the Making of the Modern World* (New York: Basic Books, 1997).

Jamie Woolf, *Mom-in-Chief: How Wisdom from the Workplace Can Save your Family from Chaos* (San Francisco: Jossey-Bass, imprint of Wiley, 2009).

Jim George, *Discourses of Global Politics: A Critical (Re) Introduction to International Relations* (Boulder, Colorado: Lynne Rienner Publishers, 1994).

J. M. Blaut, *The Colonizer's Model of the World: Geographical Diffusionism and Eurocentric History (New York: The Guilford Press, 1993).*

Johan Galtung, *Peace by Peaceful Means: Peace and Conflict, Development and Civilization* (London: Sage Publications, 1996).

John Rundell and Stephen Mennell, eds. *Classical Readings in Culture and Civilization* (London: Routledge, 1988).

Jonathan R. White, *Terrorism: An Introduction* (Singapore: Thomson Asia Pte Ltd., 2002).

Ken Booth & Tim Dunne, eds. *Worlds in Collision: Terror and the Future of Global Order* (Hampshire: Palgrave Macmillan, 2002).

Kenneth Waltz, *Man, the State, and War: A Theoretical Analysis* (New York: Columbia University Press, 1959).

Lawerence E. Cahoone, ed., *From Modernism to Postmodernism: An Anthology* (Oxford: Blackwell Publishers Ltd., 1997), reprint.

Lawerence Freedman, ed., *Superterrorism: Policy Responses* (Oxford: Blackwell Publishing Ltd., 2002).

Mark Juergensmeyer, *Terror in the Mind of God: The Global Rise of Religious Violence* (New Delhi: Oxford University Press, 2000).

..............., *Religious Nationalism Confronts the Secular* State (Delhi: Oxford University Press, 1993).

Michael Argyle, *Social Encounters: Readings in Social Interaction* (London: Penguin Books, 1973).

Michael Luntley, *Reason, Truth and Self: the Postmodern Reconditioned* (London: Routledge, 1995).

Michael E. Brown, et al, eds. *Nationalism and Ethnic Conflict* (Cambridge, Massachusetts: The MIT Press, 2001), revised edition.

Sun Tzu, *Trans. Samuel B. Griffith, The Art of War: the new illustrated edition* (London: Duncan Baird, 2005).

Nicholas Fotion, *War & Ethics: a new just war theory* (London: Continuum, 2008).

Owen Chadwick, *The Secularization of the European Mind in the Nineteenth Century* (Cambridge: Cambridge University Press, 1975).

Paul R. Brass, *Ethnicity and Nationalism: Theory and Comparison* (New Delhi: Sage Publications India Pvt. Ltd., 1991).

Peter Chalk, *West European Terrorism and Counter-Terrorism: The Evolving Dynamic* (New York: St. Martin's Press, 1996).

Peter C. Sederberg, *Terrorist Myths: Illusion, Rhetoric, and Reality* (New Jersey: Prentice Hall, 1989).

Richard Falk, et al, eds. *Towards A Just World Order* (Boulder, Colorado: Westview Press, 1982), Volume 1.

Richard Falk, *The Promise of World Order: Essays in Normative International Relations* (London: Wheatsheaf Books, 1987).

Robert O. Keohane, ed., *Neorealism and Its Critics* (New York: Columbia University Press, 1986).

Robert F. Gorman, *Great Debates at the United Nations: An Encyclopedia of Fifty Key Issues 1945-2000* (Westport, Connecticut: Greenwood Press, 2001).

R.G. Frey & Christopher W. Morris, eds. *Violence, Terrorism and Justice* (Cambridge: Cambridge University Press, 1991).

R. Scott Appleby, *The Ambivalence of the Sacred: Religion, Violence, and Reconciliation* (Lanham, Maryland: Rowman & Littlefield Publishers, Inc., 2000).

R.B.J. Walker, *Inside/Outside: International Relations as Political Theory* (Cambridge: Cambridge University Press, 1993).

Samuel P. Huntington, *The Clash of Civilizations and the Remaking of World Order* (New Delhi: Penguin Books India (P) Ltd., 1997).

Sankaran Krishna, *Postcolonial Insecurities: India, Sri Lanka, and the Question of Nationhood* (Minneapolis: University of Minnesota Press, 1999).

Sara M. Evans & Harry C. Boyte, *Free Spaces: The Sources of Democratic Change in America* (New York: Harper & Row, Publishers, Inc., 1986).

SeyyedVali Reza Nasr, *Islamic Leviathan: Islam and the Making of State Power* (New York: OxfordUniversity Press, 2001).

Simon During, ed., *The Cultural Studies Reader* (London: Routledge, 1999 reprint).

Stephanie Neuman, ed., *International Relations Theory and the Third World* (New York: St. Martin's Press, 1998).

Stephanie Neuman, ed., *International Relations Theory and the Third World* (New York: St. Martin's Press, 1998).

Terry Nardin & David R. Mapel, eds. *Traditions of International Ethics* (Cambridge: Cambridge University Press, 1992).

Thomas L. Friedman, *The World is Flat: The Globalized World in the Twenty-First Century* (London: Penguin Books, 2006).

Tracey Whitmore, *How to write an impressive CV & Cover letter* (New Delhi: Rupa Publications, 2011 reprint).

Turkkaya Ataov, *Kashmir and Neighbours: Tale, Terror, Truce* (Aldershot: Ashgate Publishing Ltd., 2001).

Walter Laqueur, *The New Terrorism: Fanaticism and the Arms of Mass Destruction* (New York: Oxford University Press, 1999).

The three features do function in a synergy as far as human universes are concerned and inform our views, opinions as well as shape them. Or even direct them. That what we call data are selective pieces and bits of information that we choose to gather, to serve various purposes. The differences between data in the physical natural world and the human cognitive universes remain pertinent. This has to do with the technology employed to collect information as well as the knowledge employed (or at one's disposal) when one seeks to collect information or data.

Thus data that speaks of the 2016 Paris Summit is different than the data that speaks of the incidents of violence that immediately preceded the Paris Summit. Both are events and both are results of multi-layered processes. Yet the nature of the Paris Summit – given its topic – makes it different of the two human events. This is because the 2016 Paris Summit dealt with climate as a factor and necessarily needed to present data collected by humans – of the physical natural world, while studying the above figure. It is doubtful if they could have done otherwise.

Data: Research, analysis & zen-cookies

Data or datum (in singular) is merely a piece of information about any given topic and/or subject. We collect data to help us do multifarious things in the human world. Yet it

Is an artifice on one hand, and not so on the other. In reality of a profound level (and some not so profound ones too) data is an artifice in how 1. it is generated. 2. it is collected. 3. it is processed, and 4. it is analyzed. We also look at other factors – especially in the social sciences – like 1. Who identifies what forms data? 2. Who collects it? 3. How is data collected? 4. What generates particular data?

This simply means the cognition that amidst infinity of data, we are constrained to make choices that the plethora of questions that we have seen make inevitable. This makes data a selective activity. This of course generates its own further data, turning data generation into a near endless process, in the contemporary human world and the social sciences.

Environmental Analysis is no different except that we have taken particular complex processes, identified their implications and used them as simplified tools to help us arrive at simpler methods of analysis of both macro and micro social processes. We have merely simplified the range of data that is needed – making what is obviously and evidently available as the basics and thus simplified the whole gamut of research. With large dollops of zen-cookies though!

Research Methodologies
1. Quantitative approaches
2. Qualitative approaches

www.ingramcontent.com/pod-product-compliance
Lightning Source LLC
Chambersburg PA
CBHW020923180526
45163CB00007B/2859